Saving Grace
...and Other Tales of Animal Encounters

Virginia Larsen

with Jocelyn Pihlaja

Copyright © 2017 Virginia Larsen

All rights reserved.

ISBN: 198183589X
ISBN-13: 978-1981835898

To the memory of Kristin Wee,

who opened her home and offered me
a quiet place in which to write

and

whose many years of wisdom and
friendship will continue to influence how I live.

ACKNOWLEDGMENTS

As with *The Book of Lurch*, which was "hatched" at the end of July 2017, I am indebted to the best publishing team one could ever wish for: Jocelyn Pihlaja, editor; Byron Johnson, cover design; and Kirsten Lindbloom, publisher. For the record, Jocelyn is my dearest friend, Byron is her super-talented husband, and Kirsten is my beloved wife.

CONTENTS

1	You've Got Mail	1
2	A Little Night Music	8
3	A Trick up My Sleeve	10
4	A Warm Trickle	14
5	A Wing and a Prayer	17
6	Chimney Sweep	23
7	Feeling the Pinch	26
8	Milk, No Honey	32
9	Her Majesty	35
10	My Personal Lizard	38
11	Perking Right Along	45
12	Saving Grace	55
13	Snake in the Grass	63
14	Well, Well, Well	66

YOU'VE GOT MAIL
Chapter 1

Part One:

One blustery late evening in October, I decided to mail an important letter.

I had just ended a 24-hour fast, my first, and had written some thoughts about this experience to a friend living far away. The point of my fast was to show God that I was serious about wanting to be of service to others in any kind of need. I had no idea who "others" might be, but I was open, curious, and confident that God would take me seriously.

Because of the wind, the rain, and the chill, I stopped to grab a knit scarf in addition to my raincoat and hat. With the letter tucked in my bosom, I sloshed to my car and headed for the post office, windshield wipers whipping at full speed.

At the drive-up mailbox, I rolled down my window and tossed in the letter. As I was cranking the window back up, I heard a meowing nearby. *Nearby?* I rolled the window back down. The sounds were coming from…inside…the mailbox! And they were more *mews* than *meows*, so I judged there was a kitten inexplicably marooned inside.

Sitting there in the driver's seat, my car idling in the frigid rain, I couldn't believe my ears. A live animal? In a drive-up mailbox? How did it get in there? The mail slot was so narrow and the metal box so dark, so cold, so scary! Even more perplexing was the larger question: why would someone do this? Was this some kind of joke? Was there perhaps a stamped tag around the kitty's neck with Aunt Ethel's rural Stewartville address on it?

I had two immediate concerns: for a frightened, trapped kitten and for my important letter. I checked the next mail pick-up: 8:00 a.m. Nine hours away – a long time for a scared feline to sit on the mail. A worry popped into my head: *Hey, kitty, please don't litter on my letter!*

Frantic about the fate of this helpless mammal – **and** the mail – I decided to drive to the police station. Before closing my window, I called, by way of offering comfort and hope, "Just wait, Kitty, I'll be right back!" As if it had a choice.

Halfway around the block, my brain skittering like a cat chasing a laser beam, I had an idea. With a plan in mind, I circled back to the mailbox, rolled down my window, took the scarf from around my neck, fed it through the mail slot, and called, "Come, Kitty, Kitty!" To my great joy, I felt a tug on the scarf. Then another. And another. A few more, and suddenly a small black form squeezed through the slot, leapt through the car window, and fastened itself onto my neck, crying, "*Mew, mew, mew*!" over and over and over again. Suddenly, instead of a plain woolen scarf, I had one that was interactive, furry, and frantically grateful. Even after I shifted the car into Drive and started to head home, the distraught kitten clung to my neck, mewing its distress.

Truly, I had never before experienced what felt like gratitude and relief expressed by a creature not having the gift of speech. Faced with this kitten's desperate affection, I was humbled. As well, I was filled with a sense of gratitude that I, of all people who could have decided to mail a letter that late evening, was the one who was chosen – yes, I felt singled out, called, selected – to perform this rescue. Even more, I was grateful for the last-minute impulse that had urged me to grab a scarf as an afterthought before heading out into the rain. My heart was full. I breathed a thank-you to God as I pulled into the driveway. Apparently, the message of my fast had been successfully delivered through the mail slot of the Pearly Gates.

Part Two:

The black cat I rescued turned out to be a female, still a kitten but old enough to be interested in birds – in a possibly predatory way. This posed a problem, as I was sharing my house and life at that time with a physically compromised and therefore vulnerable cockatiel who lived uncaged because he could barely fly.

Thus, I couldn't leave the house unless I caged the bird or shut the kitten in my bedroom. I chose the latter. I also made a big sign to post at the community college where I taught:

> **For Sale:**
> **Small Black Cat**
> **Female, beautiful, very intelligent**
> **$.05**
> **See Miss Larsen**
> **Room B-130**

The sign aroused curiosity, and before long I had interviewed several interested students and chosen Joshua, who lived 20 miles away in the next town over. Making a plan that felt very nearly criminal, we agreed to transact our business in the parking lot at noon the next day.

The following morning at 11:30, I raced home during my

office hour to fetch the cat. She jumped into my arms when I opened the bedroom door, and I felt guilty that I was about to sell her for a nickel. But I told myself that I had no choice since my disabled cockatiel had first claim, and his right to hobble from room to room made up in some way for his inability to fly normally.

I tucked the kitten in the portable wire bird cage, used only at night and for travel, and off we drove to the college parking lot. Without the complication of my bird, I would have been glad to keep her, this very alert black ball of fur, but the next best would be to secure a good home for her. I would have given her away for free, but my philosophy was that if what you want costs you something, you are more apt to take good care of it. Price was not the object; it was the principle of the thing.

Joshua met me right at noon, looking eager but sheepish. He confessed that he didn't have the money but hoped he could take the cat on credit, assuring me that he would bring me the nickel in 48 hours when he returned to campus for his next class. Having a sense of his character, willing to believe he was good for the nickel, I assented.

Forty-eight hours passed. No Joshua. Nor did I see him in the halls. Truly, it wasn't about the money; it was about honoring a commitment to invest. Equally disappointing was that I hated to be a poor judge of character – especially of a guy with a Biblical name. Just as I had been ready to release the cat from my life, I worked at letting go of my disappointment in Joshua.

One afternoon some weeks later, I was sitting in the cafeteria waiting for a colleague when Joshua appeared. Rightfully, he still looked sheepish. But along with his apology, he had the nickel and a report on the cat. In the time she had been with them, the postal-box feline had proven to be an almost spookily intuitive cat, he said.

As a result, they had named her Tara, aka Earth Goddess (Terra). In a touching moment that helped me forgive his weeks of financial laxity, he announced that he and his wife were "proud to be associated with her." One could not own a cat, he said, the way a dog could be owned, and Tara's choice to stay with them was affirming.

Years later, in an era when email had superseded traditional mail, I shared this "cat tale" with a friend. In response, she summarized: "The point of this tale is that someone cruel and small-natured did a bad thing to a helpless creature, and you – through chance or providence – entered the situation as an agent who helped to tip the balance from a tragic to a lovely ending. That kitty could have died in the mailbox, but your good hearing and nimble brain came up with an idea that 'opened the door' for the kitty to be saved.

"In some ways, she saved herself (by daring to climb), but she needed you there as an instrument to aid her. Because of that random intersection late one October evening after you wrote your friend about the serious purpose of your 24-hour fast, not only did you save a creature, but you created an opportunity for a student who was trying to figure out ways to change his own life. In this way, we are reminded that even small mercies can have an unending ripple effect."

A LITTLE NIGHT MUSIC
Chapter 2

One night, after many years of retirement, singlehood, and staying up late, I went to bed at midnight, which was early for me. I fell asleep immediately, but at some point, I became aware of a low and continual noise, a kind of Buddhist hum. I was more perplexed than frightened; footsteps would have sent me directly under the bed.

Instead, I crawled out of bed and turned my ear to the partly open window. There was no noise coming from the outside. Rather, the noise came from inside and pervaded the whole house!

"Whatever could this be?" I wondered. My breastbone was beginning to buzz from the vibrations. Should I call 9-11 and report an extraterrestrial invasion? No. I decided to check it out first. Feeling brave and wide-awake, I stepped into the hallway. I was ready to play detective and solve the mystery. The hum seemed to be coming from the living room. I turned to the right and entered the humming room. There, silhouetted against a window, was my big foster cat, Mr. Katz, sitting like a stone statue on the electronic keyboard. Now I understood the hum: Mr. Katz had evidently sat on the Power button and then slid down to rest on the G key two octaves below middle C.

I turned off the power, pulled the plug, bade Mr. Katz another good night, and went back to bed. Before falling asleep, I mused, "Is there a lesson here for me? If so, what is it? Maybe it's that one should not panic over strange sounds in the night but should first identify the source."

I had, over the years, been in several situations which resulted in an animal being rescued. So, was somebody or something rescued here? Not Mr. Katz, who was cool with warming his derrière on my keyboard. Was the rescue something more personal – perhaps my self-confidence as a single person living alone, save for the company of pets? Yawning, I pulled the covers to my chin, considered the unexpected adventures that animals had always brought to my life, and, smiling in the darkness, hummed a low G.

A TRICK UP MY SLEEVE
Chapter 3

It was a mid-summer afternoon in the mid-1990's and I, like most teachers, had the summer off. My traveling companion and I had just visited the Rembrandt House in Amsterdam and were meandering back to the center of the city, crossing bridge after bridge over the canals.

Amsterdam is ideal for walking as there is minimal vehicle traffic, noise, or pollution from motor exhaust. Like Venice, Amsterdam depends more on water than on paving stones to support its commerce and move its visitors and residents from place to place.

We were intrigued by the number and variety of permanently moored houseboats on which people lived year-round. Not a bad setup, we thought – being able to enjoy trees and flowers and pedestrians on the banks without the responsibility of gardening or putting up a privacy fence. There were potted plants galore on the decks, and we saw laundry, including underwear, drying aboard, often as colorful as any flowers.

Suddenly our attention was drawn to two men and a woman, all dressed in suits, standing alongside a canal and looking down into the water. Overcome by curiosity, I ran down the stone steps to the canal's edge and asked, in English, "What is it?

"It is a mouse," answered the woman, in English.

"Oh," I replied, in puzzlement. I was terribly curious, so I drew closer to the three.

Just then one of the men looked at his watch, and the three of them hurried off. My companion and I peered down into the water, a few feet below the stone ledge where we stood. Indeed, there, in the water, was a little Dutch mouse.

It was dog-paddling, or mouse-paddling, toward the canal's edge against a current perceptible only to a creature the length of one's middle finger. Although I caught and did away with mice who invaded my house back in Minnesota, my heart reached out to this little guy because I could imagine his panic.

I watched as he (arbitrary gender assignment) paddled doggedly (mousedly?) toward the canal wall just beneath my feet. He reached the wall and tried to grab hold of the moss on it, but the moss was wet and slippery, and the mouse fell back into the water with a tiny *plop*.

Three times I watched this small drama repeat itself with the same result, and then I, one who assumes there is a solution to every problem, wracked my brain for an idea. It came immediately: the same strategy I had used to rescue a kitten from the drive-up mailbox in Minnesota some years earlier.

I took off my cardigan sweater and, holding it by one sleeve, lowered it until the other sleeve dropped gently over the mouse. After waiting 3.5 seconds, I raised the cardigan a few inches. Looking down, I scanned the water, and what I saw delighted me: there was no mouse in sight.

Hand over hand, I raised the sweater until the damp sleeve cuff was level with my chest. I shook the sleeve. A wet mouse fell into my open palm. I had grown up handling all kinds of live creatures, including reptiles, amphibians, and bugs, so a mouse rattled me not at all. I closed my hand gently and put my cardigan back on as my companion offered me a tissue. Opening my hand, I gently blotted the sodden, pitiful thing, which I then slid into a pocket and topped with a fresh tissue so as to keep him safe until I figured out what to do. He lay very still in my pocket, which surprised me. Perhaps he had swallowed a lot of canal water and felt water-logged. Or perhaps he was too exhausted to move. No matter what, he was safe with me.

My friend and I took a boat trip through the canals of Amsterdam that afternoon while the mouse napped, after which we breached our European travel rules by eating supper at a McDonald's. Even though the cheese on the burger wasn't as good as authentic Dutch cheese, we didn't have to risk the mouse jumping out at a sit-down restaurant and getting us kicked out. Fortunately, the mouse was willing and able to eat some cheese while still in my pocket.

On the way back to our hotel, we stopped behind a three-star restaurant. I transferred the mouse from my pocket to the kitchen's window well, placed the cheese and half a cracker next to him and said good-bye, breathing a small prayer that God would keep all cats away so that this tiny, bedraggled mouse could resume his normal life.

Of all the things I experienced in Amsterdam, including the Van Gogh museum and the Ann Frank House, it's the rescue of the mouse that has remained the most vivid in my memory. I was able to make a difference in a life – even though it was "just a mouse." Even more, with an attitude that no life is unworthy, I hope I would have risked my own to help and protect Ann Frank's family if I'd had the chance.

A WARM TRICKLE
Chapter 4

In a Mayan village along the Amazon River in northwestern Peru, a young Indian mother motioned for me to sit next to her after the men had finished their blow-gun demonstration for our small group of tourists.

All the young mothers in the village were wearing skirts of dried grass with nothing on the top except for several strands of shells and beads. Many of them were nursing infants under their necklaces. I assumed this young mother wanted me to hold her baby.

Turning towards her, I held out my arms. She pried something off her bosom and attached it to mine. "It" had long hairy arms and legs, a small, light-weight body, and a tiny round head, everything covered in gray stiff hair. I peered down at the face: its eyes were shut but outlined in black, like inexpertly applied mascara. The creature had no nose, just two nostril openings, and the mouth was a wide, black line.

Suddenly, it dawned on me: I was holding a three-toed tree sloth, not a newborn but still a baby, and it had wrapped its long, skinny legs around my waist and its long, skinny arms around my neck. Its head rested between my breasts, the face turned to the left, eyes still closed. I have never wished to have children of my own, so imagine my surprise when a tender, maternal emotion began to flow from my core. Something about the physical connection inspired in me sensations that were both peaceful and protective. I didn't want the moment to end.

Then, in the midst of this gentle communion, I felt something warm above the waistband of my pants. The sloth, completely relaxed, had peed on my teal-colored t-shirt. Deeply touched, I vowed never to wash that shirt again. Some people buy keychains as souvenirs; others stock up on fridge magnets. For me, though, there could never be a better memento of my time in Peru than a t-shirt smelling faintly of sloth pee.

Although the shirt did eventually get laundered, I still have it, along with a photo of me and "my" sloth baby. They serve as reminders of an unexpected moment of connection in a far-off place. Even though I went fishing on the Amazon and caught a small piranha, and even though I allowed several Peruvian millipedes to slither up and down my arm on their dozens of fluttery, feathery feet, and even though I walked alongside a semi-domesticated black male tapir and fended off a bare-feet-obsessed red-and-blue parrot at the lodge where we stayed, and even though I climbed Machu Picchu and petted several alpacas and vicuñas, no other experience in South America came close to the feeling of that little sloth's resolute hug and the distinctive mark he left behind.

A WING AND A PRAYER
Chapter 5

One day a young fellow brought a large shoebox with air holes in it to my office at the community college. Inside was an injured dove. Apparently, it had fallen under the blade of a field mower and had thus lost a wing.

"I know you like animals," he said with what must have been hope in his voice. "We can't take care of it on the farm, and I feel sorry for it, so I was thinking you might…." His voice trailed off. He looked steadily at me. I peeked a second time into the box. The dove made a cooing sound. Its voice was strong. *Not about to die*, I thought to myself. Maybe I could handle this.

Reassuringly, I told him, "I'll do my best. Don't worry. It's good of you to care…and to trust that I would take the poor thing."

He went off to class. I made sure the lid was secure on

the box, and then I too went off to class.

At that time, I was living with Lurch, a handicapped cockatiel, who had the run – or the lurch – of the house. When I brought the new bird home with me, I was dismayed to see that it was aggressive toward Lurch. It ruffled its feathers the way a dog raises its hackles, made a cross between a chortle and a growl in its throat, and lunged at Lurch, who shrieked and shrank back and waited for me to lift him to safety. This happened a few times the first day. After that, I was careful to keep them in separate rooms at all times. What might the dove do to Lurch? It might pick his eyes out, I thought, and my blood ran cold. So much for the "dove of peace" image! Despite its image and natural beauty, it offered neither serenity nor security.

The dove's wing was not bleeding, and it didn't seem to be in pain. It accepted some of Lurch's parakeet food and sipped from his water bowl on the floor while Lurch skated at a safe distance on the kitchen counter. Clearly, I was facing a challenge. I had two disabled birds in one cozy house, one small wire cage where Lurch slept, and the shoe box. Enhancing this atmosphere was occasional bird poo plopped onto the kitchen counter or floor, where we were hanging out while I thought about what to do.

I had to smile as I strategized, imagining myself running a group home for mobility- and flight-impaired birds. That idea did not *fly* with me, but I was willing to give the dove some time to adjust to domestic life, including board, room, and the run of my bedroom, which had a door. Lurch would continue to have dominion over the rest of the house.

I decided, for practical reasons, that this dove was female and naively thought that naming her might give her a sense of family and quell her more aggressive tendencies. I was also into fund-raising for a student organization, so, combining my missions, I made this sign:

> **Naming rights, today only!**
> **Simply write your first name on a ticket,**
> **and place the ticket in this bowl.**
> **If your name is drawn,**
> **this lovely dove will be named for you!**
> **For just 10¢**
> **(Cash only)**

The next morning, I liberated the dove from my bathroom, where she had spent the night. She seemed healthy except for the missing wing, but of course not overly friendly. Why should she be? She was a wild animal, after all, and it's hard in any case to be pleasant when living with abiding pain.

I borrowed Lurch's canary cage, which he used only for sleeping and for travel, and took the dove with me to the college. Strategically, I placed the cage in the hallway outside the secretaries' coffee room and posted the sign next to it, waiting there as the secretaries passed by on their way to morning coffee. Probably as a personal favor to me more than out of a need for celebrity, every single secretary wrote her first name on a slip of paper, put it into the bowl, and gave me a dime. They were impressed, I think, that this dual-purpose project was for their participation only. I made 90¢ that day.

At 2:30, the time of the second coffee break, a handful of students and several faculty members assembled outside of the secretaries' break room. Lending weight to the moment, the president of the college showed up. I had asked him ahead of time to do us the honor of drawing the winning ticket from the bowl. The lucky winner was a secretary named Donna. She seemed quite pleased, and all agreed that the name Donna Dove had a certain euphonious quality.

However, despite a melodius moniker, Donna Dove defiantly resisted adjusting to family life. She continued to regard Lurch as an enemy to be attacked rather than as an earthbound comrade grounded by the quirks of fate. My hope of domesticating a fully grown wild bird gradually diminished, and the strain of keeping her – and keeping her away from Lurch – led me to consider finding her a new home.

Donna was a high-maintenance pet, and I could never truly relax in my own residence when she was hopping from room to room. Furthermore, there was the constant clean-up. Lurch poo on the floor was nothing compared to the sheer quantity of dove poo in the kitchen, bathroom, and bedroom. She was obviously thriving on parakeet vittles. Nearly at the end of my optimism, I needed my peace of mind restored. I suppose I could have driven to the neighboring city and purchased a large parrot cage, but they were very expensive and would have taken up too much room in the tiny house I was renting.

After I had asked around at the college for one week, with no takers, one of the students in the organization to which I had donated 90 cents took Donna Dove, in a live trap I had borrowed, to her farm, where the cranky bird would have more room to exhaust her tempers.

About a week after the "adoption," I ran into the girl who had taken Donna home to her farm. "How is Donna Dove?" I asked.
"Fine, last time I saw her," she responded as we hurried down the hallway in opposite directions. That was good enough for me.

Although I was relieved to have Donna out of my house and out of my care, I did experience a small ethical dilemma: did I have the right to pass along a "gift" given to me by another student simply for my own convenience but, more importantly, for Lurch's safety? Should I have let the secretary Donna weigh in on this since it concerned her namesake? Most importantly, should I have been willing to sacrifice my comfort for the sake of an injured creature?

I never fully resolved that dilemma, but I did know I was grateful to have my house back, to have Lurch safe, and to feel a sense of ease again. Even more, although it ultimately didn't work out, I was glad I had opened my heart to the young fellow's request that I give the bird in the shoebox a chance – and, equally, I was glad I knew a student who was willing to take Donna off my hands and give her space and freedom on her family's farm.

Sometimes the chain of people involved in deciding the fate of a child or an animal becomes complex. A good friend who is also a community college instructor made this observation: "Education isn't always about words on the board in the classroom or in a textbook – but more about the relationships that exist in the world."

CHIMNEY SWEEP
Chapter 6

During the first nine years of living in my little red house on the edge of town, small birds fell from time to time down the chimney of the wood-burning stove in the living room. Before I wised up and had the chimney capped with a screen, I rescued them via a simple procedure using a twin-size fitted bed sheet.

As soon as I heard scratching noises in the stove pipe or inside the stove itself, I fetched the sheet. Then I opened the stove door and waited for the bird to exit. Predictably, it flew straight across the living room to the big picture window, where it fluttered in vain against the large glass pane. Always, the interlopers were sparrows.

In full rescue mode, I would put my hands inside two corners of the sheet and drape it over the frantic bird. Thus swathed, it was carried gently to the front door and encouraged to fly away – which it always did without hesitation or a parting glance.

One of these sparrows, unlike the others, did not panic and flutter vainly against the picture window, pooping here and there before I could capture him in the sheet and carry him outside. Rather, he made himself at home.

I was sitting in an armchair opposite the stove one summer afternoon when I heard a slight rustling within the stove's chimney.

Accustomed to these sounds, I knew a bird had fallen down the stovepipe. I got up and opened both the damper and the stove door, fetched a twin fitted sheet from the closet, then retreated to my chair and waited. A few minutes later, a sparrow hopped out of the stove and onto the carpet. He looked me over, apparently considered me neither threatening nor interesting, and then hopped into the dining area, where there were plenty of bread crumbs under the table on the parquet floor. An opportunist, he helped himself.

Meanwhile, I quietly opened the sliding door onto the porch as well as the screen door from the porch to outside. But the sparrow did not take the obvious exit. Instead, he hopped down the hallway, past two open doors, and into my bedroom.

There, the adventurous bird encountered a three-quarter-size bed parallel to corner windows (the crank-open kind) and limited walking space between bed, dressing table, and armoire. How could a lurking human convince a sparrow to exit the bedroom, retrace his steps down the hallway into the porch, and thence escape through an open screen door to freedom?

I followed at a discreet distance. Peeking into the bedroom, I saw him fly to the corner windows, which were closed. In vain, he fluttered against them, but he did not exhibit any panic. Unable to exit there, he bounded across my bed, jumped down on the far side, and hopped under the frame. Uh-oh. I foresaw a battle between dust bunnies and a bewildered bird! But that did not happen. This bird was cool.

I cranked open one of the windows and backed away. In a moment, he emerged from under the bed, a long-lost sock snagged momentarily in his toes, and flew up to the sill. Then he turned his head and studied me calmly before flying out the window and directly to the pussy willow tree. Proudly, he perched there, fluffed his feathers, and then swooped away.

Bending down to retrieve the sock, I considered how the brief, unplanned moments of life are the best gifts. From start to finish, this sparrow's visit had been gentle and unhurried. He explored, and I followed. Neither of us had an agenda; neither of us cared who was watching. He had had an adventure, and I was entertained by a drop-in guest. Two proofs of his visit remained: one I wiped off the floor with a tissue and the other I keep in my heart to this day.

FEELING THE PINCH
Chapter 7

When I was in my mid-forties, I took an unpaid leave from the community college in Austin, Minnesota, and went to Madagascar through the Lutheran Church (ELCA) to teach English in a small village for one academic year. My intention was to do something for a group of people who could not pay me for my services. Aspirations high, my hope was that I would become assimilated quickly into the culture and become fluent in the language, Malagasy.

Adding to my excitement about this new country was the fact that Madagascar is known for many indigenous plant and animal species seen nowhere else except in botanical gardens and zoos. The lemur is the best-known example and would prove to be a memorable part of my year.

I had been in Fort Dauphin barely two weeks when a

Malagasy woman arrived at the mission house where I was living. She carried, in addition to an infant on her back and a basket of fruit balanced on her head, a woven grass cage containing a mother brown lemur and her baby. They were for sale.

It was and is illegal to buy and sell lemurs because they are classified as endangered after being "over-poached," but the missionary dentist who lived downstairs with his wife and three kids bought the pair with the intention of donating them to the nearest wild-life preserve, Berenty, about 50 miles away.

After supper, the kids brought the encaged pair upstairs to show to me and Elaine, the teacher with whom I was staying. Having read about lemurs without ever seeing a real one in a zoo, I was beside myself with excitement and curiosity.

What do little children and unthinking adults do when encountering an interesting (and cute) animal? They reach out and touch it, of course. A devout animal lover, I had no moment of hesitation: I needed to touch them. The children told me this lemur type was called "maki" and that they were always plain brown and barely noticeable among the trees, not as obvious as the raccoon-like ring-tailed lemur or the huge white ghostly "sifakas," jumping and bounding and wailing through forests at night.

This maki and her baby had the facial characteristics of all lemurs – and many cats: pointed ears atop the head, pointed muzzle with wet nose, muzzle whiskers. The digits on their front legs were like the little fingers of a squirrel or monkey. They ate by grasping food in their front paws, which were like little hands, and then transferring the morsel to their mouth. When moving, they ambulated much like monkeys, sometimes on all fours, sometimes running on hind legs rather grotesquely. And they had the monkey's prehensile tail which, in turn, made it seem logical that their favorite food was bananas!

Thoughtlessly, I stuck my right hand's little finger into the cage. The mama, sensing possible danger to her baby, grabbed my pinky and bit it! Immediately, I retracted my finger and saw teeny-tiny teeth marks in several places, oozing teeny-tiny droplets of blood. Not yet fully realizing the implications of what had happened, I nevertheless was shocked. I had meant no harm, yet my gesture of welcome had been misunderstood. Then I realized that I had done a stupid thing: I had frightened this captive mama lemur by infringing on her space, and she had done the most natural and appropriate thing to defend herself and her baby from the dangerous digit.

Bemused, I showed my little finger to my housemate Elaine, who went immediately into high alert. She ran downstairs and reported to the dentist what had just happened. In turn, he hopped onto his motorbike and zoomed over to the nearby French doctor's house. When Elaine explained the possibility of rabies from the bite, I too became alarmed. I knew that there was no cure for rabies: if one was bitten by a rabid animal, one too would develop rabies and had a 100% chance of dying from it, a horribly painful death.

About 15 minutes later, Dr. François Klein, in charge of the French hospital in Fort Dauphin, drove up on his motorbike and explained that the only way to find out if the mother lemur had rabies was to analyze a slice of her brain but that his hospital was not equipped to do that kind of test. Fortunately, he went on, his lab did have enough rabies vaccine for the required 14 daily injections. I suddenly felt very lucky. Whether the lemur was rabid or not, my chances of NOT dying were now back to 100% -- assuming I could receive the first injection within an hour.

Racing the clock, Dr. Klein then zipped to the hospital on his motorbike, packed up one dose of anti-rabies serum and a large syringe, and returned immediately to our house.

He then administered the first of the shots I would receive for the next two weeks. The serum was yellowish and viscous, requiring a fairly fat needle to allow its passage from the syringe into my belly. The transfer seemed to take forever, and it hurt! As I forced myself into stillness, I did a lot of teeth-clenching and fist clenching. To distract myself, I would count and picture the varieties of bananas I had tasted in Madagascar, beginning with a plump, stubby red-skinned cluster and ending with the mealy plantain, which had to be cooked.

There was no way of telling if I really needed 13 more shots or not, but at least I knew I was not going to die.

From that day until the series of shots was finished, I walked to the French hospital and back Monday through Friday after teaching my English classes in the nearby village of Manantantely. Saturday and Sunday, Dr. Klein came to the house and gave me the shots in the kitchen. I sat on a plain wooden chair, slipped off my flip-flops, and curled my toes around the bottom rung.

Dr. Klein administered the shots in a clockwise pattern around my navel, the result being that my belly always had several "turkey eggs" of varying sizes under the skin. I recall no other negative side-effects; I only remember that in 1982-83 wrap-around skirts were in fashion. Fortunately, I had brought two! Since my swollen abdomen made me look second-trimester pregnant, I was glad to have skirts to wear with adjustable waistbands.

The next morning, the dentist's children discovered the mother lemur dead in the cage. Who knows why? Soon after, the baby died. Many wild animals die quickly in captivity. Some die because they are full of parasites, which take over when the host does not eat and so loses the strength to keep them at bay. In this case, we had no way of knowing.

Now, when I visit a zoo that keeps lemurs, I always spend some time observing them because I feel a special attachment, which of course they do not share. By now, I have overcome my embarrassment at my thoughtless gesture back in November of 1982, which resulted in the bite and the awful shots. However, I have not let go of the lesson I learned from that quick but significant moment, and today I would set a much wiser example of how to interact with a wild animal: look but don't touch.

MILK, NO HONEY
Chapter 8

In October of 2001, during my two-week stay in Birlad, a smallish city in central Romania, I lived in a hotel with five other women from the United States. We were there as a service team through Global Volunteers. Four from our team spent every weekday at a hospital/orphanage in the nearby village of Tutova. The other two of us – Donna, an artist from Seattle, and I – gave English lessons at the school about six blocks away from the hotel.

The Tutova volunteers ate their noon meal with the Tutova staff while Donna and I walked back to the hotel for our meal and then returned to the school for afternoon classes.

Romania, like many former Soviet Union countries and developing nations worldwide, has a problem with feral dogs in its cities, even in small towns. Birlad was no exception.

On the third day, Donna and I were aware of being followed to and from the school by a canine we came to call our "favorite lactating bitch." This dog, medium-sized, was short-haired and tan in color and had an udder that would put a cow to shame. The rest of her was very skinny; her ribs and hip bones protruded from under her skin. Given her gaunt appearance, save for her mammaries, we wondered how many pups she was nourishing from her own body's resources. Quite a few, we decided.

Chagrined at this mama dog's plight, we elected to share our breakfasts and lunches with her. It didn't take long for her to identify us as a very important food source since we walked the same streets four times a day, always with food for her if we came from the hotel. Within a few days, she had become positively Pavlovian in her response to the sight of us.

For several reasons, we never touched her: she might mistake our outstretched hands and bite; she might have rabies; she might share her fleas or other parasites with us; she might become so attached to us that it would be cruel to abandon her at the end of our stay.

The morning of our departure, we brought her our last offering. Our hearts were heavy, and we weren't feeling happy at the thought of suddenly abandoning this canine mother with no one to replace us. How would she make up for our bounty after we disappeared from her life? Certainly, her pups, however many there were, were two weeks older and bigger and would require more milk and maybe solid food, yet we were leaving the lactating bitch to cope on her own.

Donna and I left Romania reluctantly, wondering if we had done the wrong thing, especially in a country that was already overrun with dogs. At the same time, we couldn't help but hope that a few weeks of good eating had made a difference not only for the mother but also for her pups. No matter what happened to that family of dogs, we took comfort in this version of an old adage: it is better to have shared even for a short time than never to have shared at all.

HER MAJESTY
Chapter 9

Because of the infestation of Japanese beetles during the summer of 2017, there were beetle bags hanging all over town, bags whose purpose was to attract these invaders into the opening of the sack, down through a narrow neck, and into the "hold," as it were, from whence they could neither crawl nor fly out and thus had no choice but to die.

We had two of these hanging from poles in our garden.

It was a late afternoon, warm and still. I was in the garden, checking on things and admiring the variety of plants and flowers. As I made my rounds, I came within two feet of a beetle bag and noticed a strange flat shape in the top part of the bag, like a dark triangle, the size of a folded dollar bill. Drawing nearer, I saw that it was a monarch butterfly, its wings closed within the narrow confines of the upper chamber of the bag.

I was horrified and wanted to free it immediately, so I reached up to unhook the bag from the pole to which it was firmly fastened with four twisty-ties. Luckily, I had my gardening shears in a hip pocket! Quickly, I snipped the bag loose, but as I did so, the monarch slipped through the narrow neck of the bag and fell onto a pile of about a million dead or dying beetles.

Once again, I was horrified, but not to the point that I couldn't think. Holding the bag by the bottom half, just under the neck, I used my trusty shears to snip the bag under the neck before reaching in and extracting the monarch by gently pinching its wings. Carefully, gently, I put down the bag, grasped a very tall grass stalk with my left hand, and hung the butterfly on the stalk so that it was suspended by its feet, upside down.

Gently it flexed its wings. Open. Shut. Open. Shut. It seemed to be gathering strength. I helped it come topside of the grass stalk whereupon it flexed its wings a few more times, as if testing to verify that they still worked. They were working better and better.

I held out my left hand. It crawled onto my palm and did a few more flexes. I happened to have my phone in my right pocket, so I retrieved it and managed to get some photos as the fragile creature flexed its wings on my left palm. "Oh, you are so beautiful," I breathed and held my palm high over my head. The monarch lifted off, fluttered higher and higher, and then flew across the street and into the neighbor's very tall weeping willow tree. Within seconds, it was no longer visible. But I knew it was there…and not in the beetle bag.

Dusk was falling, so I went into the house, still feeling euphoric but also humbled and grateful to have been the one – the only one and just the right one – to carry out Operation Monarch Rescue.

But I was left with this question: why did I make such an effort to save one monarch butterfly while doing all I could to eradicate thousands of Japanese beetles? Why are monarchs (and maybe all butterflies) worth saving but Japanese beetles not? (Is this true of all beetles in our human value system?) One species has become rare while the other has humans outnumbered by millions, maybe billions. Does rarity impart value? Both Japanese beetles and monarch butterflies, in my opinion, are beautiful to look at. But because one is elusive and the other overwhelming, my feelings about them diverge. For a single butterfly, I feel reverence accompanied by an intake of breath; for a billion beetles, I feel annoyance accompanied by a hissed, "Get in the bag!"

MY PERSONAL LIZARD
Chapter 10

While teaching English in the village of Manantantely in southern Madagascar, I had the day use of an abandoned missionary house.

I had taken a year's leave from the community college in Austin, Minnesota, because I wanted to do something for others without being paid. I lived in the Lutheran mission compound in Fort Dauphin, a city large enough to be on any map of the small island nation, and commuted by bush taxi to Manantantely Monday through Friday, a distance of about 10 miles. There, I taught English, without books, to several age groups, from the equivalent of grade 6 through grade 11.

With so many hours each day spent in Manantantely, I needed a place to relax during my breaks from teaching. Fortunately, I was able to set up a rudimentary office in one room of a huge and mostly empty missionary house near the school. Although there was no running water or electricity, I was only there between certain classes and during the noon hour. Periodically, I fetched a pail of water from the pump in the schoolyard to flush the toilet. I brought my lunch from "home." In such fashion, my basic needs were met.

On the second day as a teacher in this still-unfamiliar setup, I stepped onto the mission house's wide porch, on which were stacked many slender wooden poles, and saw something move. It scuttled under the poles. Curious to see what it could be, I waited but was not frightened – because I had read that Madagascar has no poisonous snakes or large feral animals like lions or tigers. Nothing appeared. I was a bit disappointed because creatures of all kinds intrigue me, and I wondered if something exotic might be living on "my" porch. However, I didn't have time to loiter, so I went inside to eat my lunch. My housemate Elaine had packed my lunch of two cold rolled-up pancakes, a small chubby red banana, left-over popcorn, and boiled water.

The house was unfurnished except for my office room, which had windows looking onto the porch and beyond to the school. This room had a large desk, an office chair, a bench, a round coffee table, and some bookshelves. Upstairs were empty bedrooms and some very large land turtle shells, like huge bowls. I tried to envision a missionary family with lots of kids living there year-round. Contemplating past residents, I wondered where they might have moved to and what they might be doing.

The house had very thick walls of mud brick, with stucco overlay. Thus, it remained remarkably cool most of the time, despite temperatures outside rising to well over 100° Fahrenheit from November through March during summertime in the Southern Hemisphere. All in all, there was nothing spooky about this big, empty house, and after inspecting every room upstairs and down, I settled into my office space quite comfortably. Although there were occasional scuttles outside, I did not detect any creatures living inside.

But in the coming days, I discovered that I was not alone in the house. The same creature that had skittered for cover on the porch had somehow found its way into my "office," the room closest to the pile of poles on the porch. I discovered "him" during the noon hour of my second day of teaching, the same day I'd first almost caught a glimpse of him outside. I was eating a second cold pancake at my desk when movement on the floor caught my eye.

It turned out to be a lizard, about a foot long. He was not a chameleon: he was not colorful and did not have only two toes on each foot for grasping while climbing. Rather, he evidently preferred ground level living, which "my" house provided, along with protection from any natural enemies lurking nearby.

Delighted to have company in this new place, I flicked a

piece of pancake in his direction. He attacked it immediately and devoured it before looking up to where I was sitting behind my desk. Then and there, he made the connection that we might have a future together.

The Malagasy word for lizard is *androngu*, pronounced *ahn-jung-goo*. After his first bite of pancake, this *androngu* decided that life was more interesting – and tasty – indoors than on the porch. Henceforth, he came out from under the bookcase as soon as I entered the house, positioning himself for a handout. Frankly, I was honored that he felt safe in my presence; I was not his enemy. To the extent that it was possible, we became friends. His drab coloring, protruding elbows, and bulging eyes were endearing identifiers to me.

Androngu, as I came to call him, enjoyed sharing my lunch: bits of apple, cold pancake, bread, or banana. I would flick a morsel onto the floor at least 18 inches away from where he waited, licking his chops. As soon as the morsel landed, he scuttled across the floor like a goal-oriented crocodile, pounced on his prey, and dragged it under the bookcase, where, according to the noises I heard, he devoured it with gusto.

Of course, Androngu was not house-broken. No paper, including toilet paper, was manufactured on the island of Madagascar, so it would have been the height of indulgence and wastefulness to wipe up *androngu* poo with a tissue or a sheet from my notebook. Instead, I used a big leaf from one of the trees growing next to the porch.

Actually, I felt a bit maternal, cleaning up after my personal lizard.

One day two male students from my advanced class asked to visit me in my office. They wanted to look through some of the old magazines I had brought from the mission compound in Fort Dauphin. Also, I possessed a Malagasy/English dictionary, and they hoped to look up some words to increase their vocabulary.

While Daniel and Randria were speaking softly to each other about the magazines, Androngu sidled over to where they were and, without waiting for an introduction, pooped near their feet. Then, just as quickly, he ran for cover under the bookcase.

The young men seemed surprised, not that a lizard was in my office but that I didn't appear frightened or disgusted. They asked to borrow the dictionary.

A moment later, Daniel cleared his throat and said, "Miss?"

"Yes, Daniel?"

Daniel asked, in his polite way, "This lizard, he makes poop?"

"Yes, Daniel," I assured him, "he makes poop."

"Thank you, Miss."

"You're welcome, Daniel."

Daniel and Randria asked other questions – about the English language, differences in spelling and pronunciation between British-English and American-English, and certain slang expressions in the magazines. But they had minimal interest in the lizard, for one would expect to find lizards, geckos and cockroaches in every Malagasy dwelling. Even though Andrungu was a source of companionship and fascination for me, his presence elicited not much more than a shrug from the English-hungry native students.

As the days passed, I realized the noon hour flew by much too quickly. Hoping to elicit more interactions with Androngu, one day I brought a special treat in my lunch: the drumstick of a Malagasy chicken. Malagasy chickens are skinny and always tip forward as if in a hurry. Their meat is a bit tough (no fat to speak of) but very flavorful. Once I had eaten the meat from the drumstick, I tossed it onto the floor, wanting to see if Androngu was an omnivore. He was under the bookcase, but as soon as he heard the bone hit the floor, he raced out at top speed.

Androngu seized the bone and dragged it under the bookcase. I heard him "killing" it as he thrashed from side to side, the bone ends rapping percussive noises on the hardwood floor. Then he came out with it clamped firmly in his jaws. Stopping in front of my desk, he dropped the bone and placed his front feet on it like a true victor, elbows protruding, and commenced to lick it clean in my presence. Fittingly, I was impressed.

When I left Madagascar at the end of a year, I did not say *veloma* (good-bye) to Androngu. Rather, I just disappeared from his life. He was not visible when I packed up my few office things and stuffed them into Elaine's little car for the drive back to Fort Dauphin. I couldn't leave him a farewell note. Even if I had seen him, what message could I have conveyed? Something in me felt bereft at my inability to communicate to him what a special presence he had been during this time in such a foreign country. I hoped he hadn't forgotten how to fend for himself during the nine months of our relationship. Certainly, I didn't think he had "feelings" for me as a friend. More likely, he saw an opportunity for free food and took advantage of it. He would revert naturally to self-foraging once he realized I was gone. That comforting thought allowed me to close the Androngu chapter of my life in Madagascar and focus on returning home.

I realized, however, that there is always a risk of making a feral creature dependent on a human being for sustenance. It is not natural and may cause the creature to lose the healthy fear of contact with certain dangerous humans and predators. Ultimately, although my purpose in Madagascar had been to teach, it was I who learned.

PERKING RIGHT ALONG
Chapter 11

One August when I was in my late fifties, a family with four kids and a dog moved into the house directly across the alley from mine. Initially, all I ever saw were two grade-school kids and the scruffy little dog. Its collar was hooked to a heavy chain which, in turn, was attached to a water faucet on the side of the house.

The dog had no shelter, and no one paid attention to it except the mother, who brought it food in a loaf pan once or twice a day.

It bothered me that the little dog (all 10 pounds of her) had no refuge from Minnesota weather extremes, like the heat, thunderstorms, and, in winter, sub-zero temperatures. At least she was not abused – "only" neglected. When I made my way across the alley to get a better feel for the situation, the two kids explained that

Purdy wasn't allowed in the house because their little brother Austin had asthma and was allergic to, among other things, dogs.

Weeks went by. One night in mid-October we had an especially violent storm. Awakened by rumbles of thunder, I couldn't get back to sleep; I was thinking about Purdy, alone and chained and shelter-less. Even more, as I lay in bed, fretting, I began to think about winter's arrival in a couple of months and that tiny dog stuck outside in the snow and ice, attached to the end of a frigid chain, or kept in the unheated garage.

The next morning brought sunshine, coolness, and a sense of lingering concern. Spotting the mother hanging laundry on her clothesline, I impulsively crossed the alley and approached her. "Good morning," I said. "I am your neighbor, Virginia. I wonder if you might consider selling your little dog to me for $50."

The mother looked appropriately startled by this blunt offer. "Oh, I really don't know," she replied. "Purdy was an engagement present to me from my husband four years ago." This meant the dog's entrance into their family coincided with Austin's birth, followed some time later by his asthma diagnosis.

"If you accept my offer, Purdy will be inside my house in bad weather, and that will give her a better life in Minnesota winters. You and the kids can visit her any time. Maybe you and your husband could talk it over tonight when he gets home from work and let me know in the morning."

"Okay," she said. I went home, praying under my breath that the husband would assent.

The next morning, we met at her clothesline. "I talked it over with my husband," she said. "We agreed that Purdy would be better off with you." My heart skipped a beat.

I said, "Come with me and I'll write you a check. Also, you'll see what Purdy's new home will be like."

"She isn't even housebroken," the mother said. "No need since she was never allowed inside."

That didn't faze me; my floors had long been acquainted with random deposits made by untamed animals. Without blinking, I reassured the mother, "I'm sure it won't take long if she imitates the dog I already have. She's a black cocker spaniel named Cricket."

A few minutes later, a check for $50 in hand, she left. In allowing me to adopt their dog, her load had been lightened. The kids had explained that they and Austin had a baby sister, about nine months old, who had been born with severe mental and physical handicaps. Even without a dog in her life, this beleaguered mother had plenty of burdens to carry.

So, suddenly I was the owner of one and a half dogs. I stood in my kitchen with Purdy, this raggedy terrier mix, and a host of mixed feelings. Certainly, I was happy for Purdy – but I wasn't sure about the reaction of my friend Libby, who lived 40 miles away in Rochester and with whom I shared Cricket, exchanging her every two weeks at a midway point on Interstate 90. Owning half a dog was perfect, and, outside of the impulse to save Purdy from a wretched life, I had no genuine desire to add a whole dog to my already full life. Cricket happened to be with her "other mother" that week, so neither Cricket nor Libby knew I was about to upend the balance. Contemplating the complication that was Purdy, I realized I had to make some plans!

I looked at Purdy, who was sitting on the floor and gazing up at me with a quizzical expression. As I returned her gaze, I took stock and decided there were three primary challenges facing us – everything else in due time:

1. Name change

2. Potty training

3. Getting Libby on board

First of all: the name. I dropped everything, held out my two hands, palms up, and prayed, "Dear God, please put a new name for this dog into my brain, one that sounds similar, so she won't have to unlearn her old one and adapt to an entirely new and different one. Thank you in advance."

I inhaled, exhaled, and bingo! There it was: **Perky**. How

perfect! It sounded enough like Purdy for her to respond to it right away, and really, it described her small, pert demeanor perfectly.

Next, I contemplated number two. I took Perky out on a leash and repeated the word "potty" several times. Eventually, she peed, and I repeated the word several times in a pleased tone, ending with "Good girl! Good girl!" I did not give her a treat, only praise.

The third item on my list was the trickiest. I wanted Perky to get a health check-up with Cricket's vet in Rochester, so I called Libby the very next morning. After we greeted each other, I said, "Guess what, Libby."

Neither excited nor wary, Libby issued a neutral: "What?"

"I just acquired a second dog."

Silence.

"Oh," Libby said then, sounding non-committal.

"She's a little terrier mix, and she needs to be checked out by Cricket's vet. Can I bring her over?"

"Sure," said Libby, suddenly sounding wary.

"Great," I said. "We'll be right over!"

Neither Libby nor I had ever entertained the idea of a second dog. Neither of us relished being tied down all day, every day, week after week, year after year. We were totally fine with each of us owning the idea of a dog half of the time and the reality of a dog the other half of the time. We agreed on diet and discipline and split the vet bills. It had long proven to be a perfect set-up.

I didn't have a clear plan and didn't want to be manipulative, but Cricket was getting old and developing ailments, so I was hoping that we could work out a schedule to accommodate Perky. She was, after all, very small, and her demands would be modest.

Fifty minutes later, as Perky and I stood at Libby's back door, my heart was racing anxiously. When Libby motioned for us to come in, I carried Perky through the kitchen and sat down on a dining chair with her in my lap. Libby took a good look at Perky's upturned face and exclaimed, her merry laugh spilling out, "Oh my goodness! She is the homeliest dog I have ever laid eyes on!" I didn't see what was so funny. In fact, my heart sank, for I had secretly hoped she would want to share this dog, too.

Cricket sniffed Perky and seemed to pronounce her acceptable. Leaving a disappointed Cricket behind, Libby took Perky and me to Cascade Animal Clinic in her car. We did not talk about the future, specifically whether it would include the sharing of two dogs or whether I'd be, well, stuck. I told her how I had come to acquire "Purdy" and how she got her new name. Libby's responses were appropriate, but I could tell she was on guard. Who could blame her? This little dog looked frightfully unkempt, and she smelled, too. She probably had fleas, which would end up invading Libby's nice car, and then Cricket would get fleas, too, and then everyone would be itchy, and my secret plan would be kaput.

Perky, who had been born in Missouri, had only been to a vet once – for shots and an ID chip when she was one. The Cascade vet took blood, urine, and fecal samples before asking us to take seats in the waiting room.

Before too long, the word came back that Perky was full of heartworms and other parasites, which meant that she would need to stay at Cascade for three days of observation and then remain kenneled for three weeks, coming out only to go potty and for appointments with the vet to see how she was handling the purging of her systems.

The vet explained why Perky would need to be kenneled approximately 23 hours out of every 24. The shots she got would kill the multitudes of heartworms in her heart, and they would be gradually carried away in her blood. But if she got too frisky, her heart would race and expel clumps of dead heartworm into her circulatory system. These would cause an obstruction like a massive blood clot in her heart or lung and kill her within minutes. The entire explanation was sobering.

As we sat quietly absorbing the vet's words, I felt something like despair. But then Libby attained heroic status: she offered to keep Perky for the next three weeks. I was to take Cricket home with me as initially planned while Libby pitched in to help reclaim Perky's health.

At the end of the recovery period, Perky was pronounced healthy and normal, and Libby announced that she hoped I would agree to share Perky the same way we shared Cricket. Marveling at the spirits of both dog and co-owner, I whispered "Hallelujah!" under my breath several times.

We now had options: we could trade dogs every two weeks, or one of us could have two dogs while the other had total independence. We tried it both ways. Both worked.

That November, Perky learned very quickly from Cricket to go outside to do her business. She also learned from Cricket to run next door and bark until our neighbor Neva let them in. First, the doggie duo received some graham crackers in Neva's kitchen, and then they each enjoyed some cuddle time, one on husband George's lap, the other on Neva's. All four watched TV together, first the soaps, then the local news, then news of Minnesota, the US, and the world, each viewer interspersing the tv binge with naps as needed. And so the winter passed.

At that time, Cricket was 12 and showing her age in a silver muzzle and ears. After Perky had been part of our family for five months, Cricket started having episodes much like small strokes. If she was with me, we raced to

Libby's in Rochester and drove as fast as we could from her house to Cascade. When they occurred at Libby's, she took Cricket to Cascade by herself.

As Cricket's health problems reached a peak, the vet suggested that Cricket stay overnight at Cascade. The next morning, a call came from Cascade saying that she had breathed her last during the night. Cricket had left us peacefully.

With Cricket gone, we were very glad we had a "back-up" dog. Perky missed Cricket for a while, as did Libby and I. Gradually, we became a one-dog family again, meeting every two weeks as usual at the Windmill Restaurant parking lot on I-90 to exchange the dog. We continued to agree on diet and discipline, and we continued to split the vet bills.

Mutually satisfied, we called this arrangement "Having our cake and eating it, too."

The years passed harmoniously, and then, when Perky was fifteen, she began having seizures. At first, they were moments when she froze before relaxing and carrying on as usual. Gradually they lasted longer and longer, and it became scary for Libby and me, though for Perky there seemed to be no pain involved. She usually fell asleep after such an episode and woke up feeling, true to her name, perky and good as new. Deep down, though, we knew it was a losing game.

Eventually, the vet at Cascade suggested we select a date to say goodbye to this "back-up" dog, who had become "primary" dog in our lives and our hearts. In the little Cascade sitting room dedicated to farewells, we held Perky between us. The vet knelt in front of the three of us, called Perky "sweetheart," and administered the shot that would release her to join our first shared dog, Cricket. Gathered together as we were, it was a holy moment. Within a few moments of being injected, Perky closed her eyes and slipped away. Libby looked at me through her tears and said, "I wish I could go like that." I nodded, "So do I."

There are millions of rescuers all over the world. I don't know how many feel as privileged as I do, and it doesn't matter. The point is that these creatures affect us deeply. Their lives intersect with ours – sometimes for minutes, sometimes for years, but, if we are truly attuned, their innocence, their silliness, their joy, and their mute stoicism touch us, and we are changed forever.

SAVING GRACE
Chapter 12

Early in my career, I taught in the Foreign Languages department at the University of North Dakota in Grand Forks. One November on the Wednesday before Thanksgiving break, Luigi, a dramatic 5-foot Italian colleague and an enthusiastic hunter, burst into my office, thrust a medium-size cardboard box at me, and shouted, "Heerr, Veerjeenya, theece ees forr you! Heppy Thenksgeeving!"

We in the Foreign Languages department were accustomed to random, unexpected exchanges with Luigi as he passed us in the hallway between classes. They always ended in laughter, followed by "Ciao!" as we headed for our classrooms or offices. But he had to my knowledge never before offered anyone a box – or any kind of gift. And he had been in the U.S. long enough to know that people don't exchange gifts at Thanksgiving.

There in my office, with Luigi hovering near my desk with anticipation, I shook the box gently. It quacked. I opened it, and out flapped a small duck. It was hard to say who was more startled, this wild, wounded water fowl or the naïve, unsuspecting language teacher who stood gaping at a bird on her desk. Immediately, Luigi assumed I was overcome with delight at his gift; he beamed at both duck and colleague, rubbing his hands together and showing several gold teeth in his wide smile.

Meanwhile, his "gift" showed every sign of being terrified in this foreign (French, German, Spanish, Italian!) environment by dropping a greasy deposit onto my desk followed by several more on the floor, where the bird had landed after a quick leap away from the captivity of the box. I felt sorry for the duck and even sorrier for the students' papers which had just been defiled. When classes reconvened after Thanksgiving, I would have some explaining to do.

Quickly, Luigi captured the duck, returned it to the box, closed the flaps, and identified the creature as a female "lesser scaup." He explained that he had shot and wounded her, after which she had gotten entangled in a fence. Once he had extricated her, he lost the heart to shoot her again. In a breathless moment of decision, he had thought of me – because he knew I loved animals and because I had a kind heart. All of this was explained to me in a rush of heavily accented English. Luigi then departed as quickly as he had come, and I was left holding the bag, or in this case the box.

For a minute, I was in shock. Previously, I had fostered mammals, birds, reptiles, and amphibians as pets or "boarders," but never a duck. And normally I would drive home to Bismarck, 250 miles away, for Thanksgiving, though that year I was staying in town as guest of my brother's in-laws. As I thought through possibilities and logistics, my brain raced.

At that point in the day, I had one more class to teach. While I felt bad about leaving the duck in the box, not doing so seemed far too risky, i.e. a crappy idea. At least the box had air holes.

Later, I drove home with my new housemate in the back seat. On one hand, I was feeling a bit overwhelmed and somewhat put-upon by Luigi, like an easy fix for his poor aim, but on the other hand, I was curious about this wild creature and already committed to compensating in any way I could for her bad luck. Since I had never heard of a *lesser scaup*, I would go to the public library the day after Thanksgiving and find out all I could.

Once home, I opened the box. The duck, her left wing dragging a little but not bleeding, hopped out, looked around, and pooped on the kitchen floor – every creature's traditional greeting in my household.

I felt (and was) unprepared except that I had birdseed in the cupboard, having acquired a second-hand parakeet not long before. It would tide us over for a day or two. As I rattled around in the kitchen, it occurred to me that, in a sense, I was having (a) duck for Thanksgiving!

Next, I set about making a sort of nest for the duck in a corner of the kitchen in my tiny rental house. I used an old towel and a small, oval braided rug. To my surprise, she settled herself upon it that very day. Next, I put out a shallow pan of water for her to suck through her bill and another, my only pie plate, filled with parakeet food. She tried it, seemed to smack her bill, and ate her fill.

The recently adopted parakeet, Bibi, was fascinated by this comparatively giant bird waddling around on the floor. If I hoped to hold conversations with Bibi about her new housemate, the duck would need a name. Considering her recent trauma and how close she came to appearing on Luigi's Thanksgiving platter, I decided to call her Grace.

For the rest of the school year, we settled into quite a comfortable relationship. There was never any question about keeping Grace. Who else would want her? And Grand Forks did not have a zoo. I bought a big bag of domestic poultry food: *"Good for farm ducks and geese,"* the label said.

When I went to Bismarck for a few days to celebrate Christmas with my family, I paid a 15-year-old neighbor boy to come in daily to check on Bibi and Grace and refill their food and water dishes. The boy got 10 cents extra for each duck poo he wiped up. He kept track on a sheet of paper by the kitchen sink, tallying up every little (or not so little) plop. As he and I both discovered, Grace, like all birds, could not be housebroken.

Grace never became what I'd call tame, but she allowed me to pick her up for two things: to put her into the half-filled bathtub once a week and to place her on my lap, where she would put her beak under her good wing and doze, quacking contentedly from time to time. Rocking gently with Grace on my lap was a time of communion I would cherish long after she was gone.

As a good water fowl, Grace loved the bathtub. Mine was very short, so it was easy to fill – with cool water – which I did once a week. To increase her enjoyment, I always sprinkled half a cup of "duck fodder," which floated on the surface of the water. She swam around and around, slurping and sieving and making chortling noises in her throat, never more fully herself than when paddling.

After the floating seeds and grains were mostly devoured, I would lift her out and place her on a towel to dry her feet and nether feathers before opening the bathroom door. I didn't know how she could accumulate grime, given her sheltered life, but she left a serious ring around the tub every week. However, I didn't mind scrubbing it away because I had grown to love this scrappy little thing.

Adding further diversion was the fact that, throughout the winter and spring, Grace faithfully practiced flying.

My little house consisted of three rooms in a line: medium-size kitchen (with small bathroom off it), small living room in the middle, and medium-size bedroom at the other end.

Once she had mapped out the floorplan of the house, Grace settled into a routine as she practiced flying:

She waddled to the far end of the kitchen and set her sights on the bedroom window at the opposite end of the house. Then, she revved up her motor by running at top speed and flapping her wings enthusiastically, though the injured wing was weak. Capitalizing on momentum, she then thrust herself forward and skipped first on one foot and then on the other in an effort to "lift off."

I watched from the sidelines, willing her to succeed, yet not knowing what to do if she did. Alas, her propulsion and confidence waned simultaneously, and she skidded to a halt every time, narrowly missing various pieces of furniture. If she had regained the ability to fly in midwinter, what then? Better to try in vain than to fly into walls and windows! More than anything, I admired her tenacity and the rigorous physical therapy to which she continually subjected herself.

Late that spring, I became engaged, and my fiancé and I decided on a simple June 8th wedding ceremony. As a result, the birds had to go – because my new husband and I were planning to honeymoon by driving around Europe in a VW Beetle from September through May. Thus, a week before the wedding, I planned to offer Grace to the zoo in Bismarck, where my family lived. A friend was willing to adopt the parakeet. In short order, I would be footloose and bird-free.

The day before my planned trip with Grace to Bismarck, I gave her some "play time," which I often did once the weather became warmer. To keep her close to home, I had tied one end of a 12-foot rope to the doorknob on the back door and the other end to a 5-foot extension cord. The other end of this I tied around one of Grace's ankles so that she had a full 17-feet of leeway for exercising.

After an hour or so, I went out to get her and discovered no duck on the other end of the extension cord. Overhead, I heard a flock of ducks, quacking as they flew northward from a winter in warmer climes. Just as I was preparing to give Grace away, she apparently took charge of her own fate, reminding me that she had never been "mine" to begin with. She tolerated my offerings of food and tub time, but in her heart, she never stopped yearning to be free.

I never learned what happened to that sweet-yet-wild creature, but I like to think that she suddenly received the grace necessary to join the passing flock and return to the life to which she had been born. In such a way, I accepted, not for the first time, that the animals I sheltered were often transient more than permanent fixtures – and sometimes the legacy of animals in our care is a lesson: we can love them, but we can never own them.

SNAKE IN THE GRASS
Chapter 13

Our tenth-grade biology class at Minot High School in North Dakota had a pet garter snake for the whole school year because Mr. Smith wisely wanted all of us, especially the girls, to get used to reptiles, especially non-poisonous snakes. The snake's name was Mildred.

Mildred was about 20 inches long, and she lived in a rectangular glass box perched on legs in front of Mr. Smith's desk. Even though most of the students never handled her, everyone got used to seeing her slither around in her habitat while she stuck out her forked tongue. Within a month or two, even the most squeamish in the class forgot to emit a weak "eek" when they saw her – so much a part of the class had Mildred become.

When the school year ended, I got to take her home. Why me? Of all the volunteers (three of us), I was the one who never used her to scare other girls, and I was the one who lingered at her glass cage before and after class, rapt as I looked at her and sometimes, with permission, picking her up, holding her, and marveling at the smooth, complex texture of her skin against the soft pinkness of my fingers.

I don't remember how much resistance my mild-mannered and long-suffering stepmother exhibited when I begged for permission to bring home this new "pet," but I won out, with certain conditions. Mildred would live in the garage in a special cage; she could not stay in the house for longer than ten minutes, and she had to be held the whole time.

Her new home, which Dad had put together, was made of window screening. It sat in one of our two coaster wagons and, thus, was easy to move around. I had three younger brothers, two of whom found a snake in a wagon to be great summer fun. Danny and John soon became famous/infamous in the neighborhood for taking her "for rides." Fortunately, they honored their promise to me and did not open the cage and take her out but, instead, loaded the entire operation into the wagon, hollering with excitement as their Traveling Snake Show rattled down the street.

Throughout the summer, I was very pleased and proud to have Mildred entrusted to my care. I owed my interest in and ease with reptiles and amphibians to my first mother, who had died when I was in the second grade. Caring for

Mildred felt like a kind of tribute to the woman who had birthed and first loved me. She had great appreciation for all creatures and had instilled in my brother Larry and me deep respect and awe for all wild animals.

As a creature surrounded by adolescents, Mildred was used to being handled. That summer, I wore her around my bare arm quite often. She did slither up my sleeve a few times, but she never fell off. On cooler days, I put her in a jacket pocket. Inadvertently, I startled a few adults, mostly women, but not by intention, and in general Mildred snaked seamlessly into our family life that summer.

Before I started grade 11, I took Mildred to Oak Park, near our house, and let her go. This was not an impulse. It just seemed like the right thing to do. What right did I or Mr. Smith or anyone have to keep her in a cage for the rest of her life? After nine months of earthworms in Mr. Smith's classroom and a summer of more worms and a few beetles in her cage on a wagon at our house, Mildred deserved a chance to find food and shelter on her own. I also hoped she would start a family the following spring so that one day her babies might slither into the lives and hearts of a new generation of young people – especially girls.

WELL, WELL, WELL
Chapter 14

It was nearly dusk when the men installing an egress window in our basement bedroom finished packing sand around the edge of the exit well and left. My wife, Kirsten, was inspecting the window by lamplight from the inside. I went outside and peered down the well.

To my surprise, something was scurrying back and forth across the small rocks at the bottom of it. I called to Kirsten to look. She was closer to the bottom surface and able to identify the creature. "It's a chipmunk!"

One thought occurred to me: how to facilitate its escape. I was too frail to climb down, and even if I could, no chipmunk would just jump into my hands. Even worse: chipmunks bite!

Thinking on my way to the garage, I decided on an old plan I had used years ago for rodent and kitten rescues.

My brain whirling, I went to the garage, looked around, and spied a knit hoodie and a dog leash. Thusly prepared, I went back to the egress well, tied one sleeve cuff to the leash, tied the leash to the water faucet close to the well and fed the hoodie into the well, gently, hand over hand, until the other sleeve cuff was touching the rocks on the bottom.

"The rest is up to you," I called down and went inside.

When I checked the well the next morning, there was no chipmunk.

Having been made aware of the well's potential danger to neighborhood animals, I checked it periodically for "drop-ins." After about three weeks, I stopped, distracted by other things, especially after Kirsten left on a trip and I was in charge of everything (house, garden, two dogs). My to-do list was full enough without checking to see what might have toppled into a hole. However, during Kirsten's four-day absence, I did check the egress well one time and was surprised – chagrined, really – to see a medium-size green toad among the rocks, motionless. I found a long stick under the maple tree and used it to reach down and prod the toad gently. No response meant there was no hurry to rescue it. I would just let it mummify and add it to my collection of desiccated amphibians, cicadas, beetles, etc. I felt bad, though, as though I'd let something down that I hadn't even known was depending on me.

A few days later, when Kirsten returned from Canada with her sister and pre-teen niece and nephew, she showed our guests the new egress window and its well. Eyeing his agile form, I asked nephew Dustin if he would be willing to climb down and hand up a dead toad. He hesitated, until Kirsten offered him the use of my pink rubberized gardening gloves.

He climbed down, espied the toad, and talked to it while summoning the courage to touch the corpse. "Hey! Did you commit suicide or what?" and "I'll pick you up if you promise not to move…or stink." After a fair bit of encouragement from Auntie Kirsten, he eventually bent down to pick it up.

Suddenly he shrieked. "It moved! It's alive! Oh gosh, what do I do now?"

"You scoop it up with both hands," his aunt called down, "and you hand it up to Auntie Ginny!" This he did fairly easily, but upon bending down, he made a discovery: there was a second toad among the rocks, this one looking, if possible, even deader than the first.

"Oh gosh," he repeated, "what do I do now?"

Auntie Kirsten replied, "You wait until Auntie Ginny has released Toad #1 in the vegetation next to the garage. Then you hand the dead guy up to her, so it can mummify in the sun and become part of her collection."

Dustin bent down to get it and let out a startled cry. "Oh

gosh, it moved! This one's alive, too! What do I do now?!"

While part of her wanted to suggest, "Kiss it, and see if it turns into a prince," Auntie Kirsten remained patient and suggested, one more time, "Same as with the first guy: you scoop it up and hand it up to Auntie Ginny."

The next day we got a call from Home Depot saying that the see-through well cover we had ordered had finally arrived. Kirsten picked it up and installed it immediately, thus assuring that no more critters would fall in.

It doesn't matter who does the rescuing, or how many people or creatures are involved. We all have particular parts to play in different rescue scenarios. Sometimes I am the rescuer, sometimes the catalyst, the one who sets the rescue in motion. What really matters is the outcome…and its effect on me…or on you. Could you be changed in some profound and mysterious way by becoming a life-saver – as Dustin was in the window well when his willingness to help resulted not only in saving two toads but also in boosted confidence and an understanding that his actions had impact? I daresay the answer is yes, for it is when we take notice of those around us and act compassionately towards them, whether it be a friend convalescing on a couch or a mouse fighting for its life in a canal, that we remember we are all connected, each of us an essential strand in the web of life.